one hundred one SIGNS *of* DESIGN

TIMELESS TRUTHS FROM SCIENCE

one hundred one 101 SIGNS of DESIGN

TIMELESS TRUTHS FROM SCIENCE

CARL WIELAND

Master
Books

First printing: August 2002

ISBN: 0-89051-368-6
Library of Congress Catalog Card Number: 2002105385

Printed in the United States of America.
Please visit our website for other great titles:
www.masterbooks.net
For information regarding author interviews, please
contact the publicity department at (870) 438-5288.

one hundred one SIGNS *of* DESIGN

INTRODUCTION

The world of science is a fascinating one, and true science gives humans not only enjoyable occupational pursuits — it can also dramatically boost the quality of life.

Many people get the idea that science and faith are incompatible, that somehow, the Christian faith (and, by extension, the Bible) is based on false history and false science.

We hope this handy source-book will alert you to the fact that science actually confirms the Bible each time the latter touches on matters of science. The quotes compiled in this slim volume remind us that many evolutionary beliefs are built on faulty assumptions. From mutations to racism, it's easy to see

how this false world view can harm us and the world in which we live.

Use this book to educate yourself, and to bring real enlightenment to those you come in contact with. You'll refer to it again and again.

In the United States alone, it is conservatively estimated that there are upwards of 10,000 professional scientists (the vast majority not officially linked to creation organizations) who believe in biblical creation.

That's probably about 4 years of graduating Bsc's from christian college

2

Historically, most scientific disciplines were
founded by great scientists (Newton, Pasteur, Faraday,
to name but a few) who were all creationists.

But did they believe it was created
in ⑦ days?

Real science depends on measuring or watching something happen, and checking it by doing it again.

4

There are unsolved problems and unanswered questions in the creation model, but the same is true for evolution. Billions of tax dollars are spent each year trying to solve evolution-related questions; a pittance, by comparison, is spent on real creationist research.

5

Everyone who insists there is no God relies upon evolution to explain nature without a designer.

No - i don't think they do actually.

6

Running right *through the entire Bible* is the theme that the God who consistently reveals himself therein made a good world (no death, struggle, violence, cruelty, or bloodshed). This entire universe has been cursed by God (Gen. 3, Rom. 8) as a consequence of the rebellion (sin) of the first man, Adam, against his Maker.

If the evolutionary story were true, the whole point of this gospel message would be lost, because Adam's predecessors would then have been clawing or clubbing each other to death in a world of bloodshed. It would also mean that the idea of a real, space-time fall of Adam with an associated curse on creation was a myth.

8

Overall, doubting Genesis has caused more
and more people to doubt the rest of the Bible.

Other ideas about the meaning of Genesis almost always arise, not from the Bible, but from trying to make the Bible somehow fit with other beliefs (such as the idea of long geological ages).

10 *The fossils actually show* ***signs of rapid burial,*** *not slow and gradual processes as most people believe. For example, there are countless millions of well-preserved fossil fish, even showing scales, fins, and eye sockets. In nature, a dead fish is quickly ripped apart by scavengers and decomposes readily. Unless the fish were buried quickly, and the sediments (e.g., mud and sand) hardened fairly rapidly, such features would not be preserved.*

The *evidence points overwhelmingly* to the rapid *formation of coal* as vast forests were uprooted and deposited, then rapidly buried.

12

Sorted, thick layers of up to 50 percent
pure pollen over vast areas unmistakably show the water-borne
nature of these [southeastern Australian] brown coal beds.

Researchers at Argonne National Laboratory have taken ordinary wood fragments, mixed them with some acid-activated clay and water, heated the mixture for 28 days at only 150 degrees Celsius with no added pressure in an air-free sealed quartz tube, and obtained coal. It doesn't need millions of years!

14

It is clear that the "slow and gradual" bias has prevented

the obvious explanation for the origin of coal — rapid

burial of catastrophically ripped-up vegetation

by massive watery catastrophe.

Moving water, especially a lot of it, can rapidly perform an enormous amount of geological work that most people think must take millions of years.

16

Darwin stated, quite correctly, that if his theory was true, there should be very large numbers of "in-between types" found as fossils. If the forelimb of a reptile, for instance, has turned into the wing of a bird, why don't we find a series of fossils showing these stages — part-limb, part-wing; or part-scale, part-feather?

Dr. David Raup, the head of one of the great museums in America, said that the situation concerning missing links "hasn't changed much" and that "we have even fewer examples of evolutionary transition than we had in Darwin's time."

18   *What is often not known* is that the strange
fossil creature Archaeopteryx, *often used as an example of a
transitional form between reptiles and birds (because it shares
features found in both classes) shows none of the crucial
transitional structures which would establish it as such beyond
reasonable doubt — the feathers are fully formed, and the wings are
proper wings. It has a backward-facing claw and curved feet
characteristic of perching birds. It was most definitely not, as
some would reconstruct it, a running feathered dinosaur.*

Enormous variation is possible between the bones of different types of dogs, such as Chihuahuas and Great Danes. Such variation can be selected for in only a few generations. The "selection pressure" from the rapidly changing environment after the Flood, and the break up of people (after God's forced dispersion at Babel) into small, isolated populations gave ideal conditions for the rapid isolation and enhancement of (pre-existing, created) genetic differences.

20

We now know that every living thing contains a program (a set of instructions, like a a blueprint or recipe) that specifies whether it will be an alligator or an avocado tree, for instance. For a human being, it specifies whether that person will have brown or blue eyes, straight or curly hair, and so forth. This information is written on a long molecule called DNA.

DNA, as DNA, *is biologically meaningless,* just as a jumble of letters carries no information; it is only when the chemical "letters" that make up DNA are assembled in a specific sequence or order that it carries the information which, when "read" by complex cellular machinery, controls the construction and operation of the organism. This sequence does not arise from the "internal" chemical properties of the substances which make up the DNA, in the same way that ink and paper molecules (or Scrabble letters) do not spontaneously assemble themselves into a particular message. The specific sequence of any particular DNA molecule occurs only because it is assembled under the "external" direction of the instructions carried by the DNA of the parent(s).

22

Natural selection can favor some information above others,
and can cause some of the information to be lost, but it
cannot create any new information.

Evolutionists know that mutations are overwhelmingly either harmful or just meaningless genetic "noise." However, their belief system demands that there must have been "upward" mutations on occasion. (Defects which give a survival advantage, like the loss of wings on windy islands, do not qualify.)

24

When we look at the inherited changes actually happening in living things, we see information either staying the same (but recombining in different ways), or being corrupted or lost (mutation, extinction), but never do we see anything which could qualify as a real, informationally "uphill" evolutionary change.

Matter left to itself does not give rise to such information (specified complexity in the form of a code system), so the only alternative is that at some point a *creative mind outside the system* imposed intelligence on to matter (as you do when you write a sentence) and programmed all the original kinds of plants and animals.

The original "elephant kind" may have been "split"

(by natural selection acting on its created information)

into the African elephant, Indian elephant, the mammoth,

and the mastodon (the last two now extinct).

One would expect a similar design for a similar structure or purpose **from the hand of the same designer.** *The same is true of the molecular similarities — a chimpanzee is more like us than say, a bullfrog is, so one would expect this to be reflected in its internal make-up as well, such as the structure of its proteins.*

28

Similarities can be explained in two ways — they all
had the same ancestor OR the same designer. *So their existence
can hardly be called proof for* either explanation.

Molecular biologist Michael Denton has shown
that the biochemical comparisons between the proteins of different
species, far from supporting evolution as is universally believed,
make a strong case for the existence of discrete types (or kinds)
and offer no evidence for common ancestry.

Early in the 20th century, evolutionists confidently stated that we had more than 80 organs which were useless, leftover ("vestigial") relics of our evolutionary past. One by one, functions were discovered for these, until there were hardly any left. Even the humble appendix now appears to have a role in fighting infection, at least in early life.

In modern times, human populations are seen to be increasing consistently at more than 1 percent per year. Allowing for disease, famine, wars, and so forth, let us take a much more conservative figure of 0.5 percent every year. At this rate, it would take only around 4,000 to 5,000 years, starting with eight people at Mount Ararat, *to reach today's population.*

32

In Genesis 3:14 we read, "And the Lord God said unto the serpent . . . 'upon your belly you shall go, and shall eat dust all the days of your life.'" Once again . . . *the Bible has been shown to be accurate* in minute detail. . . . There is an organ in the roof of the snake's mouth called "Jacobson's organ." This helps the snake to smell in addition to its nose. Its darting, forked tongue samples bits of dust by picking them up on the points of the fork, which it then presents to its matching pair of sensory organs inside its mouth. Once it has "smelt" them in this way, the tongue must be cleaned so the process can be repeated immediately. Therefore, serpents really do lick dust and eat it.

The alleged "problem" about Cain's wife having to be a close relative, far from being a challenge to the truth of Genesis, actually strengthens it! Since mutation-caused defects, occurring after a fault-free beginning, take time to accumulate over generations, Adam's offspring need not have feared deformities in the children of close marriages for many centuries.

34   *If human races have* split from the
descendants of those who survived such a colossal catastrophe as
Noah's flood, is it not logical to expect widespread memories of such
an awesome event in stories and legends? In fact, whether
Australian Aborigines, Arctic Eskimos, or American Indians,
virtually every tribe and nation on earth has such a flood story.

Many traditions also have accounts similar to the dispersion of tongues at Babel, but not stories of Moses' Red Sea crossing, for example, because this happened after *people separated at Babel.*

36

There are many dating methods which give upper limits

to the age of the earth and universe far less than

evolution requires. Some point to an age of

a few thousand years at most.

Contrary to popular belief, *carbon–dating* has nothing to do with millions of years (even with the best analytical equipment today, its upper limit is around 100,000 theoretical years). It is a method that can date only those things which still contain organic carbon. When the method and all its assumptions are understood and checked against real-world data, it is actually *a powerful argument for a young world.*

38

Carbon–dating of wood under lava that was erupted from Rangitoto (an island volcano near Auckland, New Zealand) indicates that the eruption was around 200 years ago. Yet, potassium-argon dating of the lava has given ages of up to half a million years!

If we take the biblical story at face value, then the notion of men and dinosaurs having lived together in the past is not so difficult. Many creatures have become extinct —it is happening even today. Extinction is not evolution, and *there is no fossil evidence* of dinosaurs having evolved from non-dinosaurs.

40

So many cultures have legends of dragons — great, reptilian beasts, featuring horns, scales, armor-plating — which are remarkably similar to the fossil-based reconstructions of dinosaurs and other extinct reptiles; yet we are told that no man has ever seen a dinosaur or a dragon. The Bible actually mentions dragons (the Hebrew word is tannin).

Consider the incredible improbabilities involved in getting the whole evolutionary scenario started in the first place. People talk as if it were somehow an observed fact — but the fact is that no one really has any sort of scientific explanation for how the complicated, information-bearing molecules required for even the simplest conceivable "first life" could have arisen without outside intelligence. And there are good scientific reasons for believing this to be impossible.

42

It's often overlooked that the properties of
a cell which make it alive cannot be explained by just referring
to the chemical properties of its building blocks, in the same way
the total properties of a car cannot be explained by the
properties of rubber, metal, plastic, and so forth.

It is hard to see logically how evolutionary selection mechanisms are of any use to the theory [of life originally arising from simple chemicals] until you have self-replicating, programmed machinery, such as characterizes all life, already in existence.

44

Are there "good" mutations?

Evolutionists can point to a small handful of cases in which a

mutation has helped a creature to survive better than those without

it. Actually, they need to take a closer look. Such "good" mistakes are

still the wrong types of changes to turn a fish into a philosopher —

they are headed in precisely the wrong direction.

The mutations which we observe are generally neutral (they don't change the information, or the "meaning" in the code) or else they are informationally downhill — defects which lose/corrupt information.

Evolutionists have to believe in
INFORMATION *having arisen by* PURE CHANCE.

The ugly aspects of nature are because it is a ruined, cursed creation, which, nevertheless, still shows remnants of its original beauty and total goodness.

48

A suggestion about the question of why God allowed sin to enter creation: For there to be the possibility of *true love between man and God,* mankind had to be created with a free will capable of rejecting that love.

Between 9 and 18 miles above the earth, a layer of ozone gas prevents most of the sun's harmful ultraviolet (UV) rays reaching the ground, and destroying living things.

50

I recall watching a nest with four baby birds. Each of the occupants, in polite sequence, pivoted its tail out of the nest and sent its dropping down to the ground below. God gave these tiny birds programmed instincts to avoid fouling their own nest.

Natural selection is really a very straight-forward, commonsense insight. An organism may possess some inheritable trait or character which, in a given environment, gives that organism a greater chance of passing on all of its genes to the next generation (compared with those of its fellows which don't have it). Over succeeding generations that trait or character has a good chance of becoming more widespread in that population.

52

Many small children are taught that "God made me." But unless this is more fully explained through the "glasses" of a robust biblical world view, the risk is that when the child later learns about the "natural" laws and processes of reproduction, it comes to see these as the "real" explanation in substitution for *the idea of God as its Creator.*

When someone asks if God could have used evolution, the answer really depends upon what they mean by "God." Most notions of "god" are mental constructs designed to fit what one would like to believe.

54

Could God have used evolution? It depends.
For the true God, the answer is no — for He cannot
lie, and He told us plainly what He did.

Rape is the latest and one of the most serious sins to be assigned an evolutionary explanation. *Despite the protests of many,* the view that rape is "natural" — to be avoided, certainly, but fully attributable to evolved instincts — is currently getting a strong worldwide hearing.

One reason put forward for saying that
Genesis is "non-scientific" is that the account is brief.
But since when does brevity equal inaccuracy?

Even though the Bible's purpose is not to teach history as such,
the history it teaches is true.

58

It is meaningless to claim that scriptural authority applies only to "religious things," since *the Christian gospel is all about real things,* the real origin, history, and destiny of man and the universe. Remove its claim to authority in the realm of science, and you are actually removing it from any relevance to the real world.

Though languages clearly change, and more than one language can arise by divergence from a "common ancestor," there the similarity with ideas of grand-scale biological evolution ends.

60

I think it's misleading to talk about any "evolution of language." Changes in language come about mostly from humanity's inventiveness, innate creativity, and flexibility, not from random genetic mutations filtered by selection. And languages studied today in the process of change appear mostly to be getting simpler, not more complex.

Languages are becoming extinct, and many have never been studied by linguists. Thus, estimates of the number of different "language families" vary, and are difficult. But they are generally in the vicinity of some 8 to 20 (commonly 12 or 13). That fits very comfortably with the descriptions [of a breakup by languages into extended family groups at Babel] in Genesis.

62   *Evolutionists have tried very hard to "link" the various language families so that they in turn point back to a common ancestor, i.e., to show that the original Indo-European and Sino-Asiatic languages themselves arose from some previous language. But their efforts have been without success. The evidence is wonderfully consistent with the notion that a small number of languages, separately created at Babel, has diversified into the huge variety of languages we have today.*

Most children's coloring books actually worsen the problem [of viewing the early Genesis accounts as real history]. Depictions of Eden's animals invariably exclude those real, once-living creatures — dinosaurs. This reinforces the idea that Genesis does not deal with real history, making it harder for the creation message to penetrate in adulthood.

64

Noah's ark is generally shown as a ridiculous-looking tub barely large enough to load a dozen animals. For grown-ups, this fairytale imagery usually springs to mind when the ark is mentioned. Such false images also make it easier for people to swallow the fallacy about the ark being unable to carry all the required animals.

The periosteum is a membrane that covers every bone, and it contains cells that can manufacture new bone. Thoracic (chest) surgeons routinely remove ribs, and these often grow back, in whole or in part.

66   *God designed the rib,* along with the periosteum. He would certainly have known how to remove the rib in such a way that it would later grow back, just as ribs still do today — without requiring any sort of special miracle. Adam would not have had any permanent area of weakness in his rib cage, but would have had, for all of the hundreds of years of his life, the same number of ribs that you and I have today.

Gouldian finches exhibit a fascinating design feature. In the young nestlings, there are two pairs of pearly-iridescent, blue-purplish nodules at the margin of the beak. In conditions of dim light, such as would occur on most occasions inside the nest, these nodules readily pick up and reflect the faint light from their surroundings. Although they produce no light of their own, they appear to "glow" in all but total darkness. Their obvious purpose is to act as guides for the parents of the youngsters, so they can unerringly find the right spot into which to place the food they bring to their offspring. The nodules are not apparent in the adult, in which they are no longer needed.

The evidence of the intelligent, wise Creator,

exhibiting plan, purpose, and forethought, pervades

even this fallen, once-perfect world. What wonders
there must have been in Eden!

The discovery of a portion of modern parrot jaw in a rock which is assumed by evolutionists to be 70 million years old has caused some controversy. Evolutionists have long believed that such "modern" types of birds had not evolved back in the alleged time when dinosaurs roamed the earth [the Cretaceous period]. Not only is the fossil in question shaped like a parrot's jaw, x-rays reveal a K-shaped impression (blood vessel and nerve tracks) identical to, and characteristic of, modern parrots.

70

Informed creationists have long pointed out that the biblical model of earth history would not only allow for the possibility of one species splitting into several, but would actually require that it must have happened much faster than evolutionists would expect.

The thousands of vertebrate species on the ark emerged into a world with large numbers of empty ecological niches. They must have split many times into new species in the first few centuries thereafter, as the bear population, for example, gave rise to polar bears, grizzlies, giant pandas, and more.

72 *We think that expanding* genetic research will likely reveal even more examples of built-in, "pre-fab" mechanisms for rapid change in response to environmental pressures. Ironically, as more such created mechanisms (very far from normal Darwinian ideas) are discovered, they will probably be misconstrued as support for evolution, at the same time as biblical Christians are exulting in their true significance.

Regarding Tyrannosaurus rex, two specialist biomechanical researchers have shown that the famous "king tyrant lizard" would not have been able to run fast. *The strength of a muscle is related to its cross-sectional area, whereas its mass is related to volume. So, as the strength needed escalates with increased weight, the mass of the muscle required increases still faster. At the size of a T. rex, chicken-type speed would require it to have an impossible 200 percent of its body weight in its legs. In short, large dinosaurs were much more likely to be prey for humans (e.g., hunting in groups, or using traps or poison darts) than the other way around.*

74 *Dinosaur expert* James Farlow, of Indiana-Purdue University, now says that if you were attacked by a charging T. rex, simply tripping it up or getting its feet somehow tangled would have been enough to smash it into a lifeless heap. Farlow and a physicist colleague have calculated that the huge beast was so heavy and high that if it tripped and fell while running, a tumbling tyrannosaur's torso would have slammed into the ground at a deceleration of 6g (six times the acceleration due to gravity). Its tiny front legs would have been inadequate to substantially break its fall.

The human eye actually discriminates better in indirect, lower intensity light, so the intervening layer [of nerve fibers, often regarded as evidence of "poor design"] acts as a filter, minimizing excessive light-scattering. It also filters the short-wave ultraviolet (potentially cancer-causing) light.

76

The simple act of walking into a room and immediately recognizing all the objects in it requires more computing power than a dozen of the world's top supercomputers put together.

Eyes in different creatures are designed to meet their differing needs. Humans need good resolution and detail, whereas a fly needs speed. We see a fluorescent lamp as flickering at 10 Hz (cycles per second) but it looks stable to us at 20 Hz. A fly can detect a flicker of 200 Hz, so a normal movie would look to it like a slide show!

Scientists are people, and **all people are hungry for meaning to life.** *All seek to fill the "God-shaped vacuum" inside them in all sorts of ways, at the same time that most of them are actively running away from the true Creator God. The true atheist who believes that all is random and purposeless is rare.*

The majestic truths revealed in the Bible about the real origin, meaning, and destiny of all things are firmly consistent with existing physical laws. To take God at His word requires faith, but not blind faith.

Most "religions," including liberal distortions
of Christianity, are man-made concepts. Most are either compatible
with, or flow from, evolutionary notions. They concern man's
imaginings about how to reach/please "god."

The gospel is about God reaching down to an utterly lost humanity. Undermine Genesis, and thus biblical authority, and the only thing left is "religion" — an empty, lifeless shell.

82

The true God cannot lie, nor deceive us about origins. He tells us, via a specific historical account, of His creation of a good world, in six earth-rotation days — ruined by sin, and still to be restored to a sinless, deathless condition. It is hard to imagine anything more antagonistic to the [usual] story of long ages of death and suffering before man.

If Darwin was right, there is no ultimate meaning or purpose to life except what we choose. You are born, you suffer, you die — that's it. Perhaps, if you're lucky, you may get recycled as organic manure — but beyond that, you're just a number that happened to come up in the great casino of the universe.

84 *A canyon* [such as the Grand Canyon] is the consequence of "natural" processes such as the way fluids erode rock. God did not "make" it in the sense of the other things made in creation week. Whatever geological structures were created in those sensational six days, the massive power of the Genesis flood, responsible for kilometers of sediment containing trillions of dead things all over the world, would have destroyed them.

Today's canyons and the like are the consequences, not so much of God's creative design, but of the forces He unleashed in divine judgment on sin at the time of Noah.

86

Darwin did not know how heredity really works,
but people today should know better. He did not know, for instance,
that what is passed on in reproduction is essentially a whole lot of
parcels of information (genes), or coded instructions.

It cannot be stressed enough that what natural selection actually does is get rid of information. It is not capable of creating anything new, by definition.

The price paid for adaptation, or specialization, is always the permanent loss *of some of the* information in that group of organisms.

Natural selection, by itself, is powerless to create. It is a process of "culling," of choosing between several *things* which must first be in existence.

90

Perhaps if evolution's "true believers" really had convincing evidence of a creative process, they would not feel obliged to muddy the waters so often by presenting this "downhill" process (natural selection) as if it demonstrated their belief in the ultimate "uphill" climb — molecules-to-man evolution.

In 1872, an attempt was made to elect Charles Darwin to the prestigious Zoological Section of the French Institute, but this failed because he received only 15 out of 48 votes. A prominent member of the Academy gave the reason as follows: "What has closed the doors of the Academy to Mr. Darwin is that the science of those of his books which have made his chief title to fame — Origin of the Species, and still more The Descent of Man, is not science, but a mass of assertions and absolutely gratuitous hypotheses, often evidently fallacious. This kind of publication and these theories are a bad example, which a body that respects itself cannot encourage."

Logically, only one belief system's truth-claims can be right. Today, unfortunately, Christianity's truth-claims are widely undermined by the belief that science has "proved the Bible wrong."

According to the Bible, all humans on earth today are descended from Noah and his wife, his three sons and their wives, and before that from Adam and Eve (Gen. 1–11).

Scripture distinguishes people by tribal or national groupings, not by skin color or physical features.

All peoples can interbreed and produce fertile offspring. This shows that the biological differences between the "races" are not very great. In fact, the DNA differences are trivial. The DNA of any two people in the world would typically differ by just 0.2 percent.

Genetic unity means, for instance, that white Americans, although ostensibly far removed from black Americans in phenotype, can sometimes be better tissue matches for them than are other black Americans.

We all have the same coloring pigment in our skin —
melanin. This is a dark-brownish pigment that is produced in
different amounts in special cells in our skin.

98

Most scientists now agree that, for
modern humans, "race" has little or no biological meaning.
This also argues strongly against the idea that the people
groups have been evolving separately for long periods.

The evidence for the Bible's account

of human origins is more than just biological and genetic.

Since all peoples have descended from Noah's family, and a

relatively short time ago, we would expect to find some memory of

the catastrophic Flood in the stories and legends of many people

groups. In fact, an overwhelming number of cultures do have

accounts that recall a world-destroying flood.

100

The accuracy of the historical details of Genesis is crucial to the trustworthiness of the Bible and to the whole gospel message. So the popular belief that people groups evolved their different features and could not all have come from Noah's family (contrary to the Bible) has eroded belief in the gospel of Jesus Christ.

One of the biggest justifications for racial discrimination in modern times is the belief that people groups have evolved separately.

For a free catalog or for more information about what the Bible teaches, contact one of the Answers in Genesis ministries below.

Answers in Genesis
P.O. Box 6330
Florence, KY 41022
USA

Answers in Genesis
P.O. Box 6302
Acacia Ridge DC
QLD 4110
Australia

Answers in Genesis
5-420 Erb St. West
Suite 213
Waterloo, Ontario
Canada N2L 6K6

Answers in Genesis
P.O. Box 39005
Howick, Auckland
New Zealand

CMI-UK/Europe Ltd.
15 Station Street
Whetstone
Leicestershire
LE8 6JS
Tel: 0845 6800 264

Answers in Genesis
Attn: Nao Hanada
3317-23 Nagaoka, Ibaraki-machi
Higashi-ibaraki-gun, Ibaraki-ken
   311-3116
Japan

In addition, you may contact:
        Institute for Creation Research
        P.O. Box 2667
        El Cajon, CA 92021

Other books by Carl Wieland

The Answers Book, with Ken Ham and Andrew Snelling (Green Forest, AR: Master Books, 1990).

One Blood, with Don Batten and Ken Ham (Green Forest, AR: Master Books, 1999).

Stones and Bones (Green Forest, AR: Master Books, 1996).

Walking Through Shadows, with Ken Ham (Green Forest, AR: Master Books, 2002).

Available at Christian bookstores nationwide

Carl Wieland

A former Australian medical practitioner, Dr. Wieland is in great demand as a speaker on the scientific evidence for creation/flood, and its relevance to Christianity. Carl has written many books and articles on the subjects of creation, evolution, and Genesis.